POV : You're in a Teen-Adult Phase

A book for shattered hearts

KOMAL SHAH

Writer's Pocket

First published by Writer's Pocket in 2022

email: publish@writerspocket.com

ISBN-13: 978-93-6083-843-0

www.writerspocket.com

DEDICATION

I'm glad and grateful that you chose to have this book in your hands right now. My only aim is to let the reader know even though teenage-adult life has happy moments which you could see almost everywhere but there is something that people miss out on noticing the vulnerable phase of that period.

We tend not to share the sad parts of our life and not express them in public or with close ones. This book will give you closure on what teen-adult individuals face during their sad phases of life. I've observed and written this book with an open heart. The aim is not to make a reader more depressed but after reading a reader may understand what goes around and be positive, support each other and make a change.

Please note - I may have not experienced what I've written. The pronoun mostly used is "she" in the book because I've been exposed and written it through my vision, there is no gender discrimination. You as a person can consider any gender of your choice while reading. The incidents in the poem are real though there are a few hyperbole statements that are given to give an effect.

I dedicate all the work I've done for you, the reader.

Remember, you can be vulnerable and come out strong by sharing and expressing yourself!

Happy reading!

With respect, care and love.

Komal Shah

CONTENTS

I thank myself for believing in me.
It's one of the best decision I could take in my life!

Appreciation Note

It was very complicated to walk on the path and trusting myself over and over again. No doubt there were hurdles to swamp but with that I got one of the promising and kindest soul to help me out throughout the day, the months and years. A remarkable thank you to Sidh Vora who is and was the backbone all the way. He has supported me from scratch, the process of publishing and releasing book. This book would have never been out if it wasn't him supporting me and believing in me more than I did to myself.

Also, a heartfelt thank you to Gauransh Chauhan for motivating, sparkling the ideas and letting me understand and believe in the process, helping me through the publishing process and definitely hyping whenever days seemed dull for the book. It was an unexpected support! I appreciate it.

1. One Last Hope

she just wished to let you realize that you were her home
where she could willingly walk.
She can't find that home anymore.
Look at her now - what do you behold?
She feels voiceless and tolerant.

She has one thing to do right now: look one final time at
his snapshots, the paragraphs, the messages, one last
time.

Her cheeks are red and she wipes out her tears as she
erased everything.
She knew it was not merciful but was for her best.
She felt the misery in her chest.
She carried herself to the power for help and spoke about
her suffering, her favorable days, and now where she has
entered hell.
She had faith - one day everything will be better than
ever at the place she wishes to be.

The days and nights she has sobbed for the soul he left
her for.
She is eyeing the mirror at herself with those bursts
streaming down her face while she is howling and
pleading with herself to hold on and to console herself
that it's not painful.
And then she said, "One last time, I hope."

2. All I Desire

Everyone wants love but all I desire is -

To decide to focus on myself for a year.
Witnessing I've been stuck somewhere for a long time;
it feels like nothing fair here.
Something is waiting for me better than this, I need to
allow aspects to go in the first place.

I have the energy to let things go and make things better,
make it happen gracefully.
All the way it's my journey, my existence, my little
ordeals in this massive world so I'll quit being the victim
and be the survivor.

I deserve everything I've been waiting for all my life
It may not be an easy path but do you observe where I'll
reach one day in small steps?
I can do it.

Everyone wants love until you decide….

3. Up In The Sky

A relationship where we instantly missed each other, after being together.
Take my heart or talk to my soul, I need to be with you in this life.

You were the gentleman who everyone wanted but I still need you in this life.
It took an afterlife to appreciate this.
I still pray for you to be here for once.

I imagine about you daily, I think about how to respect you in this universe where I can’t even see you anymore, it’s been years.
Now, I am surviving alone in the open sky at night to talk to you through the stars.
Can you listen to me? You’re the glossiest star up there - that’s where I understood it’s you in euphoria seeing me and how I am still loving you all the way.

I remember the promises, the conversations, the affection with you which I will never pass over.
Whenever there is uncertainty I stand where the incident occurred and my doubts go away from loving somebody else in this life.

I would never be afraid to stand deserted in this world for my entire life because I can feel your skin whenever I need you, I can feel your dignity.
All I do is pray for your presence again.

4. Took An Eternity

I remember when I was young I thought that
I would love somebody deeply.
At 20 I understood that affection wasn't loving someone,
It was finding a thousand paths to love myself first to love somebody.

I felt overwrought when people attempted to drag me down but
I did not lose hope and found the enthusiasm to love myself more.
Sometimes, I felt maybe I'm thoughtless but then I remember all I knew was there are millions of people who believed in loving themselves first.

I was heartbroken for myself that it took an eternity to understand this but now I think I will love myself for more than an eternity.
I finally am proud of myself one more time that I could understand myself better and better as days passed and love myself as years and years passed.

5. The Girl You Knew

The sweet, shy girl he met a few years back is now the most cold-hearted girl you could ever meet in life. She felt you were treating her as special but all she could get triggered that day was seeing him making every girl feel the same.

She was down to let anyone know what had happened. She stopped texting, she stopped hanging and later she ghosted you and came for real to be the most potent, respectful, and peaceful woman with a kind heart again. She started seeing her potential, and her respect and pulled everything up wherever she could.

Now, he misses the way she treated him like a king.
She is standing beside a gentleman with a ring.
He regrets it and she in life is open to new greets!

6. I’ll Get Over It One Day

I know it hurts sometimes.
I’ll get over it one day.

I criticized you for making me sensitive.
All the time I loathed myself for being sensitive but later little did I know I made myself sensitive in the moods of taking you incredibly and weakening my feelings to make you feel better.

I tried to enunciate in front of you my sentiments and always felt dull but I could speak everything in front of the mirror later little did I know I am the nicest soul to appreciate myself and the person who will take care of my feelings better than you.

I consumed all the time understanding you as a person but later little did I know your actions will bring this connection to end one day.
I cried and cried thinking I am the one at a failure in this connection and not you but later little did I know you’re not the kind of soul I’m into and I am free from all the toxic behavior which ceased me from respecting myself more deeply.

I know it hurts sometimes,
I’ll get over it one day.

7. Day And Night

I walk in daylight and tumble, it puts up time for me to rise.
There are a thousand breakouts on my skin which brings about how obvious and hurtful it is.

I sit at night in a dark room, it takes a lot of strength not to overthink, there are thousands of impressions in my mind, but still, my chest hurts whenever I feel something.

My eyes are red, my cheeks are wet, and I am in bed.
The warmth in the room makes me feel cool.

The floor and fences know how unbearable the fall and cries are!
If they were humans would it even take time for them to cuddle and comfort as no one could?

8. Give Me A Chance

When I Start to recollect the enjoyable days I had before the breakdowns during the phases of life,
I've been spending time independently in nature to see other creatures in the realm and understand life.
Imagining lately how everyone lives and leaves the world at their own pace,
The in-between living and leaving the world is what life is!

I'd faith I'll initiate living life as no one did after realising the in-between life.
I reckon I'll wander through the tough path to halt the rusty feeling in life and get a wonderful beginning one day.

And after years of learning who I am when I was in the healing process,
I hell knew I'd thrived and felt in between phases because I could discover myself when I was at my quietest.

9. The Dead Feelings

There was no one to lift me that day when I needed everyone the most.
The feelings were dead to me long back but still, the memories haunt me.
And now it makes sense why I still hold on to everything.

Whom should I go and tell - I was betrayed on, prevaricated, and fled for another soul which was not worthy.
Whom should I tell - I needed a justification for why it took place.

Why do I still stick and love somebody the way I've never been hurt?
My inner self asked, "How are you so fearless and how do you know how to love while you've been treated bitterly as if you were in hell?"
I had no answer. I was silent, flipped with tears.

There was no one to lift me that day when I needed everyone the most.
The feelings were dead to me long back but still, the memories haunt me.

10. The Voices In My Head

I thought I was getting better but sometimes at 2 at
midnight, I try to figure out what is wrong with you,
with me, with the world.
I stopped breathing and asked myself why am I not
enough?

The voices in my head tell me that I will never be good
enough but the one who was mistreated is me.
I'll not let these voices have any influence over me
anymore.

It's time to know my worth and to tell myself I am
enough because the one who was mistreated is me.

I tell myself my faults, your faults are a part of life.
I'll not correlate it to others or myself,
I'll stand up for what I assume in,
I'll acknowledge my imperfections,
I'll never be hard on myself,
I'll move on.

It's time to know my worth and to confide in myself that
I am acceptable because the one who was mistreated is
me.

11. The Bare Minimum

I knew you knew
We were meant to stay together forever
Like an ideal soul mate.

You said abruptly one day: It's over!
I knew you knew how wildly I was so in love with you.

Now, it's the mid-twenties with winter shots,
All I'm memorizing about you, we talked over wedding knots.
You outgrew years back and I needed closure on what went awry.

It's time for me to move on,
It will be one of the hardest times to step alone on this journey.
In life, I now go with the bare minimum and it is heavy to find, deep down that's all I need is peace over everything I've spared you for years!

12. Memories

Does it take time to squeeze in the memories?
To pick me up these years was one of the dangerous pills to swallow and absorb.
The person to pick me up this time was me.
I was not trying to be perfect but was getting better and better.

I forgave everyone who revealed to me their true colors of themselves,
My heart was pure to not give up on anyone and believed in good even though my life fell apart.
To pick me up these years was one of the dangerous pills to swallow and absorb.
The person to pick me up this time was me.

I wished to freeze the pleased moments earlier to feel good but now I started living for the little moments in life, I knew there is an after me who is going to be the happiest person out here.
I started feeling proud to conquer those memories I went through, I chose to heal.
I am here again, in this lowkey world.
I am back here.

13. The 1000 Battles

I was getting deeper with my thoughts,
I went with more specific thoughts for the betterment of me.
For a person like me who was weaker with less strength, hard on herself, could not communicate, and never complained of being hurt; god made me stand in this whole world thinking I will fight all the demons but all I could do after fighting was recreate myself with the wounds I had in my heart.

I never thought this would make me stronger until I fought 1000 times.
I promised myself to come out of this battle and get over it,
Till now after that, I chose peace over drama, truth over lies.
I believe in myself more than anyone does.
Now I know why the universe planned to push me in the battles, I am stronger than I could ever think.

14. After Things

I am vulnerable all the time after things fell apart,
It ended up being a habit.

Why is life so hard?
I feel so alone here, there is no way I should do it at the moment.
I am baffled all the time about life.
Is there any chance to forgive me to take the load for overthinking because I am vulnerable all the time after things fell apart?

I was stuck somewhere between things that I never thought I would be in.
I miss the old me who was inspired and motivated all the time.
Where would I find myself again in this huge world?
I think everything is so close but seems eternally far,
I feel nothing here at the moment, is there anyone who knows where I belong because I feel vulnerable all the time after things fell apart?

15. I Felt I Was Okay

I knew it was okay not to be okay.

Those empty nights I reorganized my thoughts under the open sky.
The only reason I found peace was the moon and stars moving.
I was allowing myself to breathe there freely,
I knew it was okay not to be okay.

Explaining the sky why nights are bliss - because of the moon and stars,
While explaining I froze there to be a part of the beauty of nature out there,
I knew it was okay not to be okay.

It was almost 4 in the morning,
The birds chirping,
The sun rising on its time,
Seeing the grass in the morning which was hiding all night because of darkness,
Seeing that adjustment of nature,
I felt I was okay!

16. I Hope

I hope someone thought of you today and appreciated the way you are,
I hope your smile to a stranger makes their day somewhere.

I hope the way someone has felt everything in life which broke them - no one faces that.
I hope no one cries over something which is not meant for them.
I hope you get the easiest person to love daily.

I hope you know this world is for everyone including you and can rule your private little world with the best people in your life.
I hope you give love to yourself.
I hope you are the priority on the list.
I hope you know you are the main character in your life.

I hope you have a kind heart for yourself and others.
I hope you are living your best life.
I hope you make yourself proud.
I hope the good aura in you never ends.
I hope.

17. The Rare Desire

I've waited for you since we have known each other,
every morning, every day, every night.

I loved you until my soul was buried by taking all the
pain in.
Do you still remember me and how crazy we were in
love, how we spent our time, how did we not fight, how
we stood together on our worst days?

I miss you as I missed you when we were apart for our
work,
I loved you as no one did and now that sucks.

You promised that you would never leave even if we
face hurdles, how could I fall for such a statement? I
replied to myself, "because you were so in love that you
did not recognize what's wrong and right or left and
right."

I will never forget how beautiful life was with you but I
will either not forget even roses are beautiful and have
thorns that hurt when we touch.
I desired the things which would destroy me in the end
and it did, it did.

18. The Best Memories

I did not sleep the whole night but still, the sun rose.
You did not bother me but my days still passed.

How do I describe what my heart wanted?
The melodious tune in my heart said, "I wished to spend time with you, to be together. We'll work together for our future."
I did not get a chance to describe what I wanted because - one morning you woke up and chose to spill the words on me by saying, "I can't do this anymore, let's part our ways!" and left me speechless without asking me if I am fine with it.

I just wanted to hug him and never let him go anywhere far from me but if he was meant to be in my life there was no chance this situation could occur.
It took me a long time to realize - not everything is meant to be in life.

The time I started perceiving good in every situation the less I was bothered in life.
It was good to know that walking away with good memories is enough and to live ahead making the best memories with someone again is more than enough.

19. My Dear Self

I did not love my body, I did not take care of myself
mentally and physically
I allowed my body to store the stress in it.
Lately, I realized it is essential to release all the stress
one by one, slowly.

I'd gone on a date with myself after regretting all my
time for being harsh on myself.
I did not know what my favorite color was, or what suits
me until I found I was busy hating instead of exploring
the things I love and suit me.

Deep in my heart, I now know it's time to know who I
am, what I love, and what is the best thing in me.
After knowing all the things, letting go of all the anxious
thoughts & building the trust in me, unfolded the real
world -
Things did change for me.

20. A Lot More

I asked for reassurance, I knew I trusted you but the
invoice in my heart made me do it.
You messed me up by stating, "How many times should
I tell you about it?"

I was stressed, I was tired of things happening between
us,
It never sounded normal anymore after that.
I'd to detach you from my routine and then from my life,
Little did I know you were having fun with me and
would leave me at my lowest point in life.

The nights I just wished for myself to get over it.
The more I did, the easier it became for me.
My life completely changed over the past years,
I will never forget to cheer!
I've ended up achieving a lot more than I could think.

21. How Did We Turn?

Our friendship will be my favorite because we messed up everything by coming into the relationship,
It was all perfect, we were talking as friends and hiding our feelings.
Called each other when we got free, shared food, shared beliefs, shared memes,
How did that turn into midnight talks with endless truths and deep secrets?
Did it even take a bang to get to know each other in a month?

1000 miles away, dreaming we will meet one day.
How did that become real?
Meeting for the first time, clicking pictures, going on a date, gifting each other, and saying the hardest see yaas!
Going back home, mentioning him in the stories, satisfying happy faces!
How did it turn into a memory one day?

Talked for months, shared the feelings, ended up in a relationship,
Did it take time to reverse everything back?
It's been a year and the love feels dull.
How did we turn into strangers again?

Our friendship will be my favorite because we messed up everything coming into the relationship.

22. A Thousand Years

We broke up because our hearts broke.
We told our ego to win this time cause it was between you vs me and problems, not us vs the problem.
At first, I did not get it but now I understand everything!

Don't forget you were my everything, we created the light in each other's life,
It hurts now, we broke each other brutally in dark days.
How many songs do I write for you and use the sentence, "it's been thousand years, waiting to apologize"

I remember thinking again,
I recognize my powers, I can make anything come true then why would I wait a thousand years for you?
I'd spend my entire life knowing you, I might love you even more than anyone.
Don't be afraid to ask someone where I've been for a thousand years.

23. You Broke Me

I regret nothing but crying for you, begging for you,
You broke me and you did not give a shit.

All I try to explain myself is to never feel the same pain again in life because
I was sorry for myself when I needed you that day; you were not there, you were gone from my life.
I was proud of myself because I went through the pain alone but never gave up
I'd lift myself, cheer up, love myself, even more, change for good, and forgive myself.

All I appreciate is that you removed yourself from my life with no signals because I was getting old to discuss this with myself again.

Now I do not give a shit, you broke me!

24. Let's Go Back

Staying at home all through august, spending time
fighting with the demons in my head,
I was so frustrated that I screamed," one day I am gonna be dead."
My parents were vulgarly cursing each other,
I stopped dreaming and did not want to step into the outside world further.

How could I not say the toxic environment which demolished my younger self brutally that I was living my whole life traumatizing, memorizing them daily,
I wondered what would it feel like to be an adult when I was young,
Now while I'm 20, adulthood has just taken a turn over and started to show what life is - I fear and gear up for another day, another month, another year without thinking about today.
Staying at home all through august, spending time-
fighting with the demons in my head
I was so frustrated that I screamed, "one day I am gonna be dead."

I've learned a few of my life lessons that were unexpected but my inner child says, "let's go back to the dreams where we have a perfect family when I was 10 and never come back here."
I wish I could go back there but now I want to be strong and independent in this world.

The flaws and directions I received were hard to walk in life alone and again staying at home all through august, spending time fighting with the demons in my head,
I was so frustrated that I screamed, "one day I am gonna be dead."

25. One Day

You will miss me someday,
You will even miss my voice,
You will miss how I cared for you in this ruthless world,
You will miss how I loved you unconditionally.

You will miss our bond one day,
You will miss every single thing we did together.
You will miss how I did not let you feel down at your worst,
You will miss the girl you abandoned.

You will miss the brightest days we had,
You will miss seeing me daily
You will miss everything related to me,
You will miss me someday.

26. She

She did not want to look dumb again, cry over silly things again, and be hurt again.
She has already felt the pain where she was numb and tired all the way.
It was all okay when she cried with an open heart knowing she will heal by taking out the pain,
The worst part was she looked at herself in the mirror with tears, thinking everything went wrong and had failed in life like it was an end to everything.
It was a different pain when she did not cry anymore, she just accepted what went wrong all the way.

She was never insecure until things started pointing out to be different in the situation.
She asked just for your attention, running out of her patience.

And now when she is broken into pieces -
Nothing makes her happy anymore,
Nothing makes her scared anymore,
Nothing makes her close anymore,
Nothing crosses her mind anymore.

She learned to walk away,
She allowed herself to grow in peace,
She never looked back,
She never regretted it because she did not want to look dumb again, cry over silly things again, and be hurt again.

27. For The Moment

Whatever I wanted to say, I whispered a thousand times in front of the mirror.
I admired blinking my eyes with a decent smile, my hair flipping, my words having meaningful sentences.

But I had me in front of me while listening in front of the mirror.
Whatever I wanted to say, I whispered a thousand times in front of the mirror.

How fast things move, the only moment I could click was now me crying over,
I wanted to be proud of myself for all the darkness I went through and chose to not give up.
I lost the freedom of light and space for walks,
The nights were changing and people were strangling.

I told myself, "hold for a moment, slowly for the moment."
And that's where things started to fall into place.
Hold for a moment, slowly for the moment.

28. You And Me

The silence is powerful if you hear me carefully.
Let the silence bring you close to me one day.
It's been a long I haven't seen you,
It was the last time we said goodbye to each other.
Since that life has been different.

I hope you search for me even if you hang out with different people
Still, if you don't find me anywhere, put the wings on your back the wind will bring you to me.
I was feeling heavy for leaving everything for the universe to decide,
I felt lighter because I knew you will stay with me even though right now we aren't together,
I secretly thank you for choosing me over and over.

Hear me, you can come back from everything!
We are inseparable, we will meet again soon.
I'm waiting for the universe to give me a sign so I can reach out to you until then
I hope you search for me even if you hang with different people.
Still, if you don't find me anywhere, put the wings on your back the wind will bring you to me.

29. The Life I Desired

The whole universe was by my side,
I had the power to create the life I desired!
I was just afraid of- no one would correct me if I was walking on the wrong path.
That feeling killed me inside and I was deadly alive.

I was stuck somewhere, I was not sure how to go about it.
Suddenly someone showed up and raised my life as no one could.
The energy and universe were by my side,
I was now just afraid of - may that person stay in life forever because that's what an angel is.
A person who gave an aura of heaven on earth.
I found that person!
I found the life I used to desire!

The whole universe was by my side,
I had the power to create the life I desired!

30. My Home

My thoughts sink at night around me, darkness in the room thinking about you.
I am baffled as to who you are as an individual.

One day these nights won't chase me, I will have an answer.
You've shown me the person you aren't but I still believed you're a person from heaven!
I've become a person whom you don't like anymore; you've made me die somewhere within us.
Death didn't scare me but your words did!
Death did not scare me but walking alone on the streets and finding answers did scare me.

Now, I want to go back to simpler times when you did not exist in my life, I felt safe there,
I've lost a good bond but I even lost the beautiful soul in me that believed in love.

I could relate the moments to what they meant. Life changed, I changed!
My soul has settled from the chaos suffered.
The silence in my soul now brings me back to my home.
After decades I now can feel at home.

31. Till Then Let Me Love Myself

Someday, somebody will love me again,
Someday, I will love somebody again.
Till then let me love myself a little bit more.

I will find my comfort zone again in this rush-full world,
I will find my peace while walking on sand and falling
for the beautiful sunset.
I will sigh over small things so there are no worries to
put everything on my shoulder.

I will be on the path of healing and I will find the one
who embraces little things in life,
I will be in search of living a life and unexpectedly
maybe I will find someone who will love me,
Till then let me love myself a little bit more.

I have no language to describe love, I've jotted down my
feelings of mine in a safe book.
I wish one day I'll find someone who will read the book
which I've tied with a thick thread hanging on a hook.
I've spent my time knowing who I am as an individual
and I hope the universe gives me a chance to know how
I am as a couple.

Just a little more time, I've come a far way searching for
my person,
I hope my person finds me too.
I will wait for a while, it's worth the time because
someday, somebody will love me again,

someday, I will love somebody again.

ABOUT THE AUTHOR

Komal Shah is a 19-year-old writer who boosted her career in writing in the year 2020. She is now ready to go with her first book and is more inclined to further improve and use her skills, emotions, and creativity to make her career in writing.

Writer's Pocket

Writer's Pocket is a publication house established in 2016. We began with the aim of providing a better publishing platform for aspiring writers and budding poets.

The publishing industry in India (and around the world, to a great extent) is always something of a mystery even to the writers themselves. We are working on making publishing more accessible to everyone.

So far, we have helped over 3,000 writers turn their dreams into reality by publishing the books and continue to do so. By doing so, we also provide some of the best content by Indian writers to the readers.